Chasing the *Sun*

Chasing the Sun

A journey around the world in verse

Compiled by Sally Bacon
*in association with
the Poetry Society*

Illustrated by Valerie Littlewood

SIMON & SCHUSTER
YOUNG BOOKS

For

E.J.B.   M.E.B.   V.M.S.S.   P.A.L.W.

Thomas & Camilla

This anthology has been compiled by Sally Bacon on behalf of the Poetry Society. We would like to thank every contributor for his or her contribution to this collection. Royalties from the sale of this book will go towards furthering the Poetry Society's work in promoting poetry in Education.

The Poetry Society
22 Betterton Street
London WC2H 9BU

This collection first published in Great Britain in 1992 by
Simon & Schuster Young Books
Campus 400, Maylands Avenue
Hemel Hempstead, Herts HP2 7EZ

Printed in Great Britain by St Edmundsbury Press Ltd,
Bury St Edmunds, Suffolk

British Cataloguing in Publication Data available

ISBN: 0-7500-1212-9

Contents

AMERICAS

ARCTIC REGIONS AND FAREWELL...

Foreword

Any of you who have ever flown a long distance will know that when you fly from west to east, you fly round the globe and into the rising sun. This anthology enables you to embark on a similar journey, cheating time to encircle the globe through its poetry.

This book's journey begins in the British Isles, at the start of time: Greenwich Mean Time. From there we will travel from west to east, moving through Europe, Africa, Asia, Australasia, South and North America and the Arctic.

However, you need not chase the rising sun in an easterly journey. This is also a collection to be dipped into, with countries and continents to be selected or returned to at will - especially if you ever have the chance to visit them!

The collection is structured by each of the five continents (plus a polar region), but not every country has been included: the aim is to give you a substantial taste of each continent through a variety of its countries. The poets included here come from many places: a large number from Britain, some from America, Australia, Chile, Guyana, Jamaica, India, Malaysia, Pakistan, and others. Many of the poems are new, commissioned for this anthology, and nearly all the poets are writing today, ranging in age from 11 to over 70. A small few are writers from the past, whose voices are particularly evocative or summon distinctive tales, rhymes and myths from their respective cultures, cultures that should not be forgotten.

The poems are not always a description of a particular place or landscape; there are legends and folk tales, personal experiences, glimpses of history, and authentic voices, such as those of the Innuit, or the Araucano Indians. A country is sometimes seen from the standpoint of exile within it, or from exile within another. The wildlife of each continent also provides rich inspiration for many poets. Fact and fantasy, legend and reality, people and place, all merge in this particular global journey. The variety of experience is reflected in the variety of verse: rhyme, non-rhyme, internal rhymes, shape poems, dialect poems, metaphors, funny poems and songs can all be found within these pages.

This anthology both chases the sun and cheats time: you can follow your own path of discovery, freed from any earthly constraints, dipping and hovering as you please. Mapping this journey out myself has been a rare, pleasurable, and informative experience, as each day brought new countries and new poems to my desk. Whatever the route of your journey through this collection of poetry from around the world, enjoy it - both through the poems and through the discoveries to be made within them.

Sally Bacon, 1992

The Song of Chief Koruinka

The whole earth is one spirit,
we are a part of it.
Our spirits cannot die.
They face changes, certainly,
but not extinction.
We are all one spirit,
just as there is only one world.

Araucano Indian from Chile
Translated from a Spanish version by Roger Garfitt

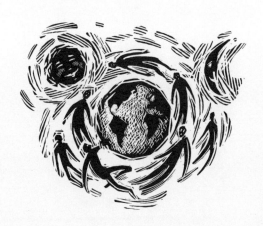

EUROPE

Ireland

To some the map of Ireland stretched
on an atlas is a skull –
a sheep's perhaps, or else a goat's,
with a knobbly great brow.
But others see a cow's head
gazing lazily out to sea
across the broad Atlantic,
chewing the cud of history.
My father's cows carry a world
of mobile information,
their own maps inked in on their sides
moving through modulations.
Their smell's the smell of earth, and warm;
their clumsy weight jostles against me
but the milk of mildness fills their veins,
their eyes speak only pity
as they go about their work
churning the bright emerald country.

Jill Townsend

Mountain Peak

I galloped my horse to the peak,
and stood, looking down.

The hills unfolded like a ruffled blanket,
under which was sleeping, God.
Perhaps it was his leg
that made the ridge
chasing along to the sun
near Carn Fflwr.
Perhaps his head
was Dibyn Du, that place my horse loved.
I had to get off,
unsaddle and bridle her,
and she crumpled on the turf
and rolled;
waving her legs at the view
and kicking her white heels above her
till she had almost touched the low sun.

God was lying under there,
and I stood on the bedpost,
and watched his changing breath
over the land.

Harriet Earis

Village School

A stile, a field,
some dozen cows
and then the church.
A muddy dyke,
some silver roach
and just below the bridge
a sharp-toothed pike
which lurks alone
for small unwary stragglers,
whispering doom.

The school, one room.
Beneath high-windowed stone
fixed smiling in her chair
the kindly Mrs Mullins,
large in blue and black
with neatly-curled hair.
From nine to twelve
and later on till three
she calls our fate
and welcomes all
on ample knee.

A scratch of slate,
a shuffle here or there,
a child in late;
chalk-dusted autumn
clouds the air.

At last a break. Wait
unwillingly for bottled milk,
cool in its rattling crate,
then under teacher's watchful eye
lace-up for play.
Scarves, coats and hopscotch
when the weather's dry
and crying at the gate for home
under a grey Lincolnshire sky.

Judith Nicholls

A Song for England

An' a so de rain a-fall

An' a so de snow a-rain

An' a so de fog a-fall

An' a so de sun a-fail

An' a so de seasons mix

An' a so de bag-o'-tricks

But a so me understan'
De misery o' de Englishman.

Andrew Salkey

From the Loch

Wetless, clean green, too day, too sun,
bubbling breeze chokes snout;

the roof lakes, not enough –
a sniff of wet cannot last me.

This air-place ripples with spies,
their flash-boxes mutter at discovery.

They send a hard pike to worry me:
it snarls in an unwet, windy breath.

I sink into mountain-dark,
swill down in storms of ancient water,

coil my mile-long spine into
a crude pot: simmer.

Lois Beeson

Mermaids

Fower and twenty mermaids,
Wha left the port o'Leith,
Tae tempt the fine auld hermit,
Wha dwelt upon Inchkeith.

Nae boat, nor waft, nor crayer,
Nor craft had they, nor oars nor sails;
Their lily hands were oars enough,
Their tillers were their tails.

Anon, from Fife

Evening, Albufeira

Day slips its anchor
and cruises into grey
of night. Roofs slide
from pink to black.
Chimney pots, like
petrified lace, are
embroidered on the sky.
Bells mark the dogwatch
with tinny tongues and
the still air comes
alive with starlings.

They swing and loop,
swirling like locusts
into the rusted branches
of the tallest tree
in town. They jabber
and gossip, filling
the square with jangled
discord. At some secret
signal they settle and sudden quiet conquers
the evening streets.

Moira Andrew

May Music in Castille

Below in the street, the music began
Of voices, mandolin, accordion, guitar,
That every midnight celebrate the May.
I was in bed, too sleepy by far
Yet again to listen to the minstrels play
Upon sweet mandolin, accordion, guitar,
So my eyelids closed as the melody ran.

But when the music stopped in mid-beat,
Voices and mandolin, accordion, guitar,
And the dumb-struck minstrels went their way,
And in the sky was no summer star
But storm and thunder to see out the May
And the voices, mandolin, accordion, guitar.
I rose for the rain. It strums in the street.

Ted Walker

Swallow Tails at Combourg, Brittany

I didn't care about the magnificence
(well, guide-books don't like to say "depressing gloom")
of the French castle with its pointy turrets
(like you see in Scotland), the one where
a famous writer whose name even begins with Chateau –
spent a lonely childhood more than two hundred years ago.

I didn't care about all the other tourists
staring upwards at windows and walls
with cameras instead of faces.

What made it special was the butterflies
I'd never seen before, waltzing across the grass,
big-wing partners, all creamy with
black designs, and long tails tipped with sky –
pairs of them cavorting and twirling across lawns
as brown as toast, buttery wafers,
wavers in twos, saying *"Bonjour!"* and *"Au Revoir!"*
as they danced their way out of all the photographs.

Rodney Pybus

The Day of the Annual Firework Display: Angles-sur-l'Anglin

Five francs purchases
a picture postcard
of the water mill
refusing to be budged
by the river.

But on the day
Of the annual firework display
Brakes are released,
Sluice gates opened
And the wheel

Locks.

Men discuss strategy.
Jackets are discarded;
Hands, moistened with spit
Force iron bars
Between the spokes.
Women and children
Climb onto the paddles
And wait;
Riders of this fairground attraction.
Old men watch from the bridge,
Shout advice
And recall days when
It was a real watermill.

Men heave down,
Women and children
Bounce their weight
Against the wheel's immobility.
Bars bend,
Paddles shudder,
Trapped stones crack
Rivets threaten to burst.

With a splintering scream,
The wheel gives in,
Shrugs off its passengers and
revolves.
A moving picture showing
For one day only.

John Coldwell

Pompeii 24th August, AD 79

The giants are sleeping now
under a hot land
where the grey snow
has yet to fall
and cover all
with its dying dew.

The city is silent now
under a haze of blue
till the pedlar's cart
on the stone-clad street
calls the early few
for pot or shoe
and the slave from sleep.

The hillside is sunwashed now
where the lush vine
and the olives line
the summer's slopes
of the giants' home
in an August dream
that has almost gone.

The gods are sleeping now
unaware
by the temple walls
and market stalls
of the city square...

And an ashen cloud
shrouds the breathless crowd
as the grey snow falls.

Judith Nicholls

A Boat's Mooring Ring
at Kallikratia

A ring-pull on the pier.
No-one is looking,
So I rip off the lid of the land.

Just as I'd guessed.
Sardines.

Simon Pitt

Death by Sacher Torte*

There's a churchyard in Vienna where
nine graves lie side by side by side.
A respected old Viennese Baker
and his full eight wives. The
old Baker was famous for his
wonderful chocolate cake,
for the puddings and the
strudel, and the pies
he could bake. Nobody
remembers them now
and you have to
peer very hard
at the graves
to read the
writing
that's
left:

The respected Viennese Baker, fed them all to death.

Elizabeth Seagar

**Sacher Torte is a rich, round chocolate cake, originally
made at the Sacher Hotel in Vienna.*

Conjurer on Charles Bridge, Prague

Is it illusion that revels
on the wildly glowing eyes
Of his audience which holds its breath,
And cheers and claps and sighs?

> Or is it the magical gleam of chance
> In his music, merriment and dance?

For he can make Moravian wine
From an old black hat and a magic sign,
And conjure to superb applause
Bohemia glass and drinking straws.

Is it illusion that revels
In the ever-changing night?
Is it tricks that mystify,
Stratagems that delight?

> Or is it the wonderful wand of truth
> He wields in hands of life and youth?

A rumour has it he set free
The spirit of democracy.
Was it contrivance or a spell?
Illusion? Magic? Who can tell?

Ben Rice

Skiing to Voikka

Beneath a sky manuscript-blue
my skis skitter on spun sugar
melting in March sun...

Spruce-shadows violet as bruises
stain the snow,
birches droop lustres of ice –
their minute janglings
tease my ears.

Taking the short cut home
over the Kymi river's width
I fancy, deep in winter's hard-core,
I can hear numbed waters stir,
and beehives at the forest edge
under their hats of snow
hum in their sleep.

Sheila Simmons

St Petersburg, April

A land of snow-filled fairy tales
    and cupolas of gold,
palaces of powder blue
    and princesses of old,
of wild, harsh and frozen wastes
    and sheets of snow so cold

that the rivers freeze solid.

The sun sets over a river twinkling
    with ice, breaking now
and splintering on a course to open
    sea. The cupolas glisten
and the princesses of old look on
    as the ice tries to chart new waters

quickly, before it melts.

Elizabeth Seagar

Topkapi

I am the sultan. Jewelled, I sit on jewels.
My head bows with the weight of jewels.
My fingers curl open with the weight of jewels.

They bring me a bowl of emeralds the size of figs
To play with if I want to, and curds
to eat with spoons so diamonded
They rasp my lower lip.

I have a candlestick
With 6666 diamonds. The British Queen
Has sent me the jewelled order of her garter.

One day I will throw myself into the Bosphorus.

John Fuller

AFRICA

Out in the Desert

Out in the desert lies the sphinx
It never eats and it never drinx
Its body quite solid without any chinx
And when the sky's all purples and pinx
(As if it was painted with coloured inx)
And the sun it ever so swiftly sinx
Behind the hills in a couple of twinx
You may hear (if you're lucky) a bell that clinx
And also tolls and also tinx
And they say at the very same sound the sphinx
It sometimes smiles and it sometimes winx:
But nobody knows just what it thinx.

Charles Causley

Drought

Sun hot
Hasn't rained
No water
Walked miles
But water's mud
River's dry
Can't bathe
Can't drink
Brown grass
No grass
Skeletons stare
From cracked earth

And then one morning
Without a warning
The sound of rain
A stranger tapping
Pitter pattering
Onto our rooftops
Into our pails
Giving birth to streams
Filling our rivers
Feeding the cattle
The sound of rain

We're all smiling
My father is hugging my
Mother
Children running naked
Mouths open towards the Gods
We're all laughing
Me forgetting to hide
The gap between my teeth.

Accabre Huntley

I am Surma*

I AM SURMA
his painted body says,
with lip plates and stick fights
we'll keep our tribal ways:

paint patterns snaked in spirals
with fingers chalked and watered,
daub red and yellow ochre
on torsos, and hindquarters!

I AM SURMA
roam freely through the forests,
raise my crops and cattle
in mountains far from tourists,

marry many SURMA wives
whose lips are split and plated-
the largest plate a bride can wear
is how her beauty's rated.

I AM SURMA
fight off the enemy
when BUMI and DIZI
invade my territory,

settle local arguments
in dinga-donga battles
with sticks - this way we SURMA
solve grievances that rattle.

I AM SURMA
his painted body says,
with lip plates and stick fights
we'll keep our tribal ways

Gina Douthwaite

* *South-western Ethiopian tribe*

Lions

Near an ancient standing Baobab tree
the lion sits with burning mane.
He looks all around
but makes no sound,
in the heat of the African plain.

Behind, in the grey and cooling shade,
the rest of the pride is lying.
After the kill
they have eaten their fill
and now sleep the safe sleep of the lion.

Tomorrow they will awaken refreshed,
as a new day breaks over the plain,
and they'll sleekly rise
with death in their eyes,
to start the hunt over again.

Robin Mellor

Rhinoceros

God simply got bored and started doodling
with ideas he'd given up on, scooping off the floor
bits and bobs and sticking them together:
the tail of a ten-ton pig he'd meant for Norway,
the long skull of a top-heavy dinosaur,
the armour-plating of his first version of
the hippo, an unpainted beak of a toucan
stuck on back to front, a dash of tantrums
he'd intended for the Abyssinian owl, the same
awful grey colour he used for landscaping the moon.

And tempted to try it with the batteries,
he set it down on the wild plains of Africa,
grinned at what he saw and let it run.

Matt Simpson

Giraffes

Beyond the brassy sun-stare where each shade
Crouches beneath its substance at mid-noon
The tall giraffes are gathered in a glade
Grazing the green fruit of the midday moon.
Patched with sienna shadows of the jungle
In pencil-slender attitudes they stand
Grotesque in camouflage, each curve and angle
Merged into the backcloth of the land.

Circus creatures of a poet's dreaming,
Secure on stilts they seldom need to run,
Keeping silent watch on hunters' scheming,
Moving unseen, unheard, are swiftly gone.
Strange genesis in which the substance seeming
The shadow is the secret of the sun.

Phoebe Hesketh

In a Kenyan Garden

A lizard, dinosaur in miniature,
Blue as a cornflower, stands sentry on the path.
Mousebirds run in the trees, peep between branches,
Or swing like big commas on the telegraph wires.

Taller than any man, the massive leaves
Of a banana tree droop and begin to rot.
The rains have come and autumn has begun
But this afternoon the garden is a slow oven.

Like a small golden harlequin or highwayman,
A black-masked weaver bird watches me while I write,
Then flies to the banana tree and delicately begins
To tease away one fibre with his beak.

He braces against his legs and twists and tugs
Till he has freed a twelve-inch length,
Flits to his village tree and cleanly threads
The new strand into the round dome of his nest.

All the hot afternoon he works, stripping the leaf,
Crafting through miraculous knowledge a perfect sphere,
One nest among a hundred on that tree,
Where, when the sun has disappeared, he'll rest.

Gerard Benson

Lechwe*

We're sure
they really think
they're birds!

They spend most of the day
with us
the pelicans, ibis, herons and ducks
eating the same weed
wading the same marsh
cooling their hooves
in a docile and sensible way

Then suddenly – they lay
their horns along their backs
and take off
bucking, bounding through the swamp
they scatter spray
and leap aloft
trailing their legs as they have seen us do

We're sad to see them go
strung out on the horizon like a frieze
    although we're sure
    they really think
    they're birds!

Sue Cowling

*Lechwe are a type of water-antelope to be found in Zambia. They
are now an endangered species.*

CLUCK

GRRR

HISSS

MOO

Aardvark

Ever heard
an aardvark
bark?

Miaows and birdcalls
all mill to its grist

OINK

TWEET

South Africa's
leading
veldtriloquist.

Roger McGough

MIAOW

BAAA

WOOF

GRRR

In South Africa

Just as the white might go sunbathing,
Letting light darken them,
Surely a black moonbathes?
At midnight, in moonglasses,
Thousands must sneak out,
And lie on the beaches
In the light of the moon,

Trying to absorb that peculiar silver,
To become pale as milk,
Leaving no coke cans or orange-peel

For the white to stumble on,
Arriving at dawn,
Burning to darken.

Helena Echlin

ASIA

Grave of a Princess

Between the hills of Hindu Kush
and vale of Amu Darya
a princess lies in templed tomb
where tribesman worshipped fire,

where traders on the great Silk Route
paid tolls in precious stones,
in treasures from the Orient
which now surround her bones.

Her hollowed eyes stare from a skull
adorned with crown, collapsible –
like trees with leaves in flakes of gold
slipped in a headband – flat they'd fold
for, being a nomadic wife,
this suited well her way of life.
Once raven hair had been festooned
by pendants linked like mobile moons,

a necklace hewn from ivory,
pearl beads with hearts of turquoise,
a bracelet like an antelope
and sewn on shrouds around her loins

gold spangles, disks – and ancient coins
are showered like confetti.
Her fingers, ringed with treasures, clutch
at combs of ebony,

a Chinese mirror laid to rest
upon her jewel-encrusted breast,
a pot of silver filled with oils –
her beauty secrets sealed by coils
of serpent. Princess well prepared
for journeying lay undisturbed
for centuries. She's almost gone
to lands beyond Afghanistan.

Gina Douthwaite

A Harvest of Wheat

All day the sounds of scythes
Cutting stalks. Our hands sticky
With juices, our arms heavy
With swathes of wheat.

All day in the blazing sun.
Our backs arched, eyes focused
On the sharp blade and the stems,
Slicing and gathering systematically.

All day in a kind of communion:
My father reciting the Koran;
My brothers and cousins exchanging
Stories and jokes. Our lives

Inter-mingling, growing around words.
Above us, the crows cawing all day.
By evening there are bales of wheat
Scattered in an open field.

The women near the edges make
Nan bread. The scent of dough
Baking comforts our exhausted bodies.
Embers float up into the navy dark sky.

One by one stars begin to glimmer.
We navigate ourselves toward Mecca.
My father's voice rises between us.
His words crumble in my moist mouth.

Tariq Latif

Day by Day I Float My Paper Boats

Day by day I float my paper boats one by one
  down the running stream.
In big black letters I write my name on them and
  the name of the village where I live.
I hope that someone in some strange land will find
  them and know who I am.
I load my little boats with shiuli flowers from our
  garden, and hope that these blooms of the dawn
  will be carried safely to land in the night.
I launch my paper boats and look into the sky and
  see the little clouds setting their white
  bulging sails.
I know not what playmate of mine in the sky
  sends them down the air to race with my boats!
When night comes I bury my face in my arms
  and dream that my paper boats float on and on
  under the midnight stars.
The fairies of sleep are sailing in them, and the
  lading is their baskets full of dreams...

Rabindranath Tagore

Dancing the Anaconda[*]

A n a c o n d a s
hissper "Conga!" through a jungle (not the Congo).
Twisting round, along, then round, bough and
branch are danced around:
so smooth, except a bulge or two, where a
not-so-quick-step bird (or beast) or two, groove
to a graver tune.
A n a c o n d a s
hokey-cokey quite a few.

A n a c o n d a s
growing longer.
Rivers offer no restriction to choreography's
constriction; the list of practised tactics
includes ballet aquatic.
"Come, we conga like a conger to apocalypso frogs,
or maybe rumba numbers that bop Orinoco hogs."

If you hear nocturnal rocking,
when snake charmers should be curling tight,
it must be
A n a c o n d a s
sleepwaltzing, through those tango-tangled
forests of the night.

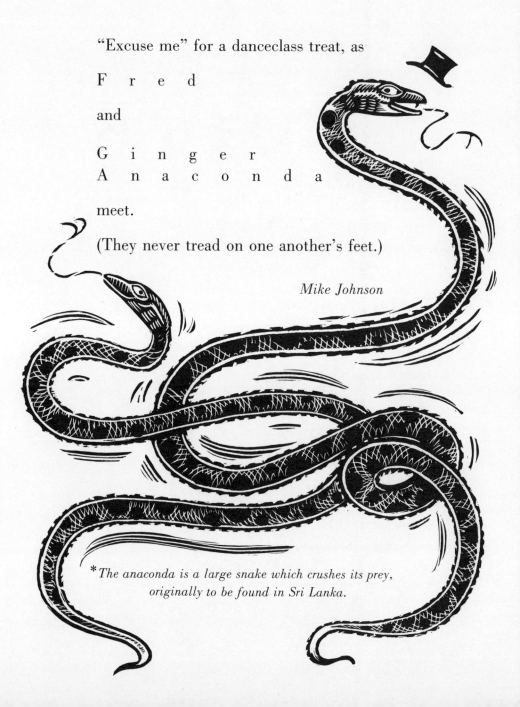

"Excuse me" for a danceclass treat, as

F   r   e   d

and

G   i   n   g   e   r
A   n   a   c   o   n   d   a

meet.

(They never tread on one another's feet.)

Mike Johnson

*The anaconda is a large snake which crushes its prey,
originally to be found in Sri Lanka.

The Not So Slow Loris*

The slow loris
                objected
                                to her name!
Well, she liked *loris* but not *slow*.
She was a primate too!
                Who was man
to bandy names about?
                What did he know,
sun-lover, long pig!
                Let him stick
to cockroaches and kangaroos.
He didn't say *slow tortoise*.
                He made her sick!

The slow loris
                sat on a grave
                                and fumed!
She paid no attention to the moon
or the stupid stars -
                man's stuff!
She wanted to go
                into Rangoon
and complain.
                She wanted man
to change the dictionaries.
She wanted apologies.
                She had no plan.

Matthew Sweeney

*The Slow Loris is an Asian primate with grey or black fur and large eyes, and it is
distinguished from the Slender Loris by its heavy build and the slowness of its movements.

Durianimal*

The durianimal
is an amazing beast
(the word is Malaysian
for "unusual feast")

Low in calories
and good to eat
an odd combination
half-fruit, half meat

In taste and texture
beyond belief
imagine pineapple
and rare roast beef

(To vegetarians
they remain a puzzle
some refrain
while others guzzle)

Growing on trees
until mature
they drop from the
branches
and crawl on the floor

With yellowish leaves
two legs and two arms
they live in the shade
of the durian palms

But not for long...

Considered such
a gourmet treat
their lives (like their bodies)
are short and sweet.

Roger McGough

The Durian is a Malaysian fruit. Oval in shape, it has a hard, prickly rind, and luscious cream-coloured pulp with an overpowering odour. It is considered by some to be a rich delicacy.

The Doll Festival*

Lighted lanterns
cast a gentle radiance
on pink peach blossoms.

Third day of third month.
Mother brings out five long shelves –
black lacquer, red silk.

On the topmost shelf
we place gilded folding screens
and the two chief dolls.

They are Emperor
and Empress, in formal robes:
gauzes, silks, brocades.

On the lower steps,
court ladies with banquet trays,
samisen players.

High officials, too,
kneeling in solemn stillness:
young noble pages.

Fairy furniture –
dressers, mirrors, lacquer bowls,
bonsai, fans, braziers.

Should the royal pair
wish to go blossom-viewing –
two golden palanquins.

Third day of third month.
Our small house holds a palace –
we are its guardians.

Lighted lanterns
cast a gentle radiance
on pink peach blossoms.

James Kirkup

*Long ago, the Japanese used dolls to drive away evil spirits.
On March 3rd, Japanese children celebrate the Doll festival by
creating a royal court, consisting of a set of 15 dolls on stands
draped with red cloth.*

In the High Mountains

This mist
has spun itself adrift
from lakes and rivers;
it spreads below us
fine as porcelain,
a clean white plate.

Soon a pigtailed man
in a blue boat will sail by
to paint blue willow trees,
blue water, blue birds to fly,
a bridge to wander on;
we'll be his dreaming lovers.

Irene Rawnsley

AUSTRALASIA

Haiku Calendar: Southern Version

In the sun's oven
New Year bakes to perfection
iced by the ocean.

February nights
with softness you can touch
like possums in gumtrees.

March dries orange leaves
on gnarled, blackened trunks after
the bushfire summer.

Like a kangaroo
this April afternoon lies
stretched in the cool dust.

From cold May mornings
the warmth of Autumn soars in
canopies of blue.

Like an owl's feather
the year's first snowflake settles
into dusky June.

July holds its breath
in silent valleys muffled
by the drifted snow.

Cloud-splitting August
flashes silver rivers down
the sky's thunder mountains.

After winter rain
September like an emu
treads so warily.

October sunset:
a wedge of black cockatoos
calls wheel-oo wheel-oo.

November sunrise
feathers greying sky with pink:
galahs on the move.

Flaming December:
sulphur-crested cockatoos
dip the year in gold.

Barrie Wade

Great Grey Kangaroo

In the dry, hot dawn of the Outback
the Great Grey leaps an empty creek bed.
With a dancer's grace, it lifts its face
into the sun that lies ahead.

Ancestral spirit of the Dreamtime,
it glides past a Stringybark Tree,
and men will trust, as its feet kick red dust,
that they too will always be free.

The Old Spirit stops in the noontime,
stands high on legs and tail,
looks at the ground and turns around,
then moves on, a dream in full sail.

Like smoke it passes a billabong;
distant rocks are hazy in view,
where once, on the shore, long years before,
men drew pictures of kangaroo.

The squabbles of flying foxes
mark out the end of the day,
and a solitary man walks across the rough land,
in the path of the ancient Great Grey.

Robin Mellor

The Bunyip*

Oh, came you up by the place of dread
(West red, and the moon low down)
Where no winds blow and the birds have fled
And the gum stands dead and its arms gleam white,
And the tribe sneaks by with a stealthy tread
In the ghostly light, in the ghostly light.
Brave Worralang went one grey nightfall
(A woi! woi!) where the grim rocks frown;
He came no more to the camps at all
(Skies dark, and the moon low down).

As we came up by the gully side
(Deep dusk, and the moon low down)
A dingo whined and a curlew cried
And the reeds replied as in hushed affright
Where tall brave Worralang screamed and died
In the ghostly light, in the ghostly light.
For the Thing lurks there in the haunted place
(A woi! woi!) where the pool is brown,
Where lost ones vanish and leave no trace
(Day dead, and the moon low down).

Oh, go not by near the bunyip's lair
(Stars dim, and the moon low down)
Or tip-toe past and beware, beware
The dark pool snare and be set for flight,
For things of terror have happened there
In the ghostly light, in the ghostly light.
And in the gunyas we crouch and hark
(A woi! woi!) where the dead men drown
The monster's bellow across the dark
(Stars gone, and the moon low down).

James Devaney

*Aborigine name for a fabulous marsh monster in Australia.

The Dancers

To a clearing
in the foyer
at the Gallery
of Art,
and a chatter
of spectators
waiting for the show
to start,
five young men, black,
naked, dotted
white and daddy-long-
legs thin
out of forty
thousand years of
dreamtime came lightfoot-
ing in.

    Ssss! hissed the dancers from Arnhem Land.

And a primal
stillness fell as
when arose the earl-
iest sun,
each dancer an
emblem painted
on rockface, or scored
in stone.
With an unpre-
meditated
seemliness they took
the floor,
staring sightless
as is lightning
through a bronze by Hen-
ry Moore.

     Ssss! hissed the dancers from Arnhem Land.

To an insect
buzz of music,
snap of sticks, high nas-
al whine,
touched with brown and
saffron ochre,
and their teeth a yell-
ow shine,
five young men came
barefoot, dancing –
the sun halting in
its climb –
effortlessly,
forwards, backwards
through the littoral
of time.

     Ssss! hissed the dancers from Arnhem Land.

Beaded and in
feather bracelets
to the hoarse-voiced didge-
ridoo,
they were the emu
and echidna,
swirling snake and kang-
aroo;
razoring this and
that way sharply,
swifter than the bush-
fire flame,
each a demon,
each an angel,
each a god without
a name.

    Ssss! hissed the dancers from Arnhem Land.

Suddenly the
dance was ended,
clocks took back the Mel-
bourne day,
and it was as
if the dancers
melted like a mist
away.
In the restaur-
ant I saw them,
serious, and at smil-
ing ease:
five young men in
T-shirts, jeans, with
pavlovas and five
white teas.

    Ssss! hissed the dancers from Arnhem Land.

Charles Causley

Once in a Lifetime, Snow

Winters at home brought wind,
Black frost and raw
Grey rain in barbed-wire fields,
But never more

Until the day my uncle
Rose at dawn
And stepped outside – to find
His paddocks gone,

His cattle to their hocks
In ghostly ground
And unaccustomed light
For miles around.

And he stepped short, and gazed
Lit from below,
And half his wrinkles vanished
Murmuring *"Snow..."*

A man of farm and fact
He stared to see
The facts of weather raised
To a mystery

White on the world he knew
And all he owned.
Snow? Here? he mused. I see.
High time I learned...

Les Murray

New Zealand Shore

This is where the last moas*
blundered into the sea

from snares and shouts in the wood
from the fleshtight drum;

drawn out from the aeons, hilltops
of ragged fern and bog hollows

haunts of old power, pursued
by a new thing, a bird in plumage

of heaven with death in its wings.
Legstumps and spread toes slipping

on estuary mud, their great necks waving
from side to side, they straddled the first

wave, blinked salt from their eyes, and stood
facing the forest, and the ring of hunters

who closed with nets and spears, and
the slow feathers of sunset

dropping beyond sight or memory.

Hilary Llewellyn-Williams

**The Moa was a flightless bird, now extinct, that was
three metres tall.*

Hine-Ruhi*

when you, my Hine-ruhi
took unconditional flight
that monday morning
turning, turning all
my days into night
at last i knew why
we call our mondays black

once you were gone
out, out went the light
leaving no one
to tempt another dawn
from the horizon
to end my endless night

Cecil Rajendra

*In Maori legend, Hine-ruhi was the woman whose beauty
caused the wonder of dawn to reappear.*

The Coming

The rumours started
in the time of our fathers
and of their fathers. A volunteer
setting out from this place
wandered for generations among people
of no blood, the tribes of the West...

        Now there are reports
from Porgera. He comes trailing dust
in a yellow car along the Highway.
We can read the signs, we know this car
has a special diet. In the night
when all are asleep, we will open up
his secret mouth, and feed him from our garden.

E A Markham

AMERICAS

Carnival in Rio

1

car-ni-val car-ni-val car-ni-val
this is car-ni-val

Peacocks with feathers of the rainbow,
wings' spread held all day;
the robes of kings drag yards behind,
heads-above-their-own crowns sway.

car-ni-val car-ni-val car-ni-val
this is car-ni-val

Bare-backed, straight-backed Princes
strapped to the steel pan and the bass.
Princess in tresses of diamonds,
glitters as she rattles her waist.

car-ni-val car-ni-val car-ni-val
this is car-ni-val

Freedom fighters in battle dress,
the spirit of their banners in their dance;
tinselled toddlers on shoulders,
wide-eyed in the wildest of dreams.

car-ni-val car-ni-val car-ni-val
this is car-ni-val

2

We reach for the rainbow,
drape it across our streets,
wrap ourselves in its colours.

come let we wine and grine no girl
carnival not once a year
come let we wine and grine

We catch the morning bird's song
in steel pan and bass sounds,
beat out those songs all day.

come let we wine and grine no girl
carnival not once a year
come let we wine and grine

We bake, fry and drink like old time:
the right amount of spice, the right peas,
the best rice; cane rum and sasparilla.

come let we wine and grine no girl
carnival not once a year
come let we wine and grine

3

Steel drums rattle and thump,
the beating players jump as they play.
We follow the rhythm as close as wasps
their queen; sing the same few lines
in a sweet drone.

Following, you have to dance each step:
put a foot forward, shake the body,
swing the arms from side to side,
thrust out the hips and smile,
if you're not laughing, part those lips
for breath if nothing else.

You're rubbing up another body
in front, one rubbing you from behind;
two on your sides bump to your hips'
pendulum swing. Wherever your arm stretches
for balance you grab a shoulder
or waist; when they jump, you take off too.

So they carry you along,
they, in turn, carried by the rhythm,
partly yours and everybody's.
It's ownerless really,
like this stomping ground called Earth
and mother, you can't see for people.

Never mind street names, they're postal
conveniences. Life is a honeycomb
made to eat from; just sort out the sting
from the honey and the choreography
comes with ease, grace; so rock on,
but mind that island in the road!

Fred D'Aguiar

Curandero*

Curandero, with ancient brews,
will banish ailments from Peru:

with ceremonial sorcery
sick sufferers of agony
in body, soul, or in the mind
will evil spirits leave behind,
will have them cast out by his skills.

Curandero can cure all ills:

to skull, extracted from a tomb,
his magic potions and perfumes
are offered first, as though respect
for ancestors will then protect

Curandero from spells he makes,
inhales - and then hallucinates.

He chants out charms and pants in prayer,
attacks the apparitions there
with swords especially selected
to deal with demons, so detected.

Throughout the night he'll thrash and flail,
in trance, until whatever ailed
his patient has been exorcised...

Curandero, exhausted lies.

Gina Douthwaite

*The Curer

Breeze of Ghosts

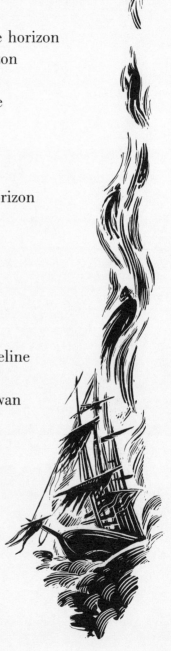

Tall ship hanging out at the horizon
tall ship blistering the horizon
you've been there so long
your sheets and decks white
in the sun

what wind whispers you in?

Tall ship creaking at the horizon
your capital long gone
your crew in the cabin
drinking white rum
their breath spiralling

what wind breathes you in?

Tall ship tilting to the shoreline
past Spanish palms
tall ship coming in like a swan
in the mid-day sun

what wind blows you in?

It is the cool
wind of the morning
stirring my masts
before the sun
burns it to nothing,
they call it
breeze of ghosts.

Helen Dunmore

Back Home

Back home

       the sun does greet you with a smile
       creep up the bed clothes until
       you open your eye
       Bright and hot
       The sky blue and clear
       Every day does fill you with cheer

Back home

       is all type of mango
       banana, orange and plum
       growing in we garden
       ripening in the heat
       Any time you want you can
       pick some and eat

Back home

       the sea at we back door
       I could step out the house
       and run down to bathe
       listen to the waves when I in bed
       They does soothe me good
       They does help me sleep

Back home

       But I not back home
       I here in England
       where the sun not so hot
       and the fruit not so ripe
       and the sea does chill your feet

Back home

       is just a sad-sweet memory

Amryl Johnson

Pods Pop and Grin

Strong strong sun, in that look
you have, lands ripen
fruits, trees, people.

Lands love the flame of your gaze.
Lands hide some warmth
of sun-eye for darkness.

All for you pods pop and grin.
Bananas hurry up and grow.
Coconut becomes water and oil.

Palm trees try to fly to you
but just dance everywhere.
Silk leaves of bamboo rustle wild.

And when rain finished falling
winds shake diamonds from branches
that again feel your eye.

Strong strong sun, in you
lands keep ripening
fruits, trees, people.

Birds go on tuning up
and don't care at all –
more blood berries are coming.

Your look strokes up all
summertime. We hear streams running.
You come back every day.

James Berry

Seven Wishes

Why can't I be the band that binds your forehead,
so close to your thoughts?

Why can't I be the nub of sweetcorn
you shred with your wildcat's teeth?

Why can't I be the turquoise round your neck
warmed by the storm of your blood?

Why can't I be the thread of many colours
that slides through your fingers on the loom?

Why can't I be the velvet tunic
over the ebb and flow of your heart?

Why can't I be the sand in your moccasins
that dares to stroke your toes?

Why can't I be your night's dream
when you moan in the black arms of sleep?

Pueblo Indians of New Mexico

Sargasso*

I
was
born
free in
hanging
gardens.
My cradle
of weed
was swung
beneath
a green
canopy
warmed by
father sun
rocked by
mother sea
as it was
in the be-
ginning
when time
too was
young.

I
was
fine
as a hair
and clear
as glass.
A current
ruffled us.
Millions
set out,
twisting
east two
thousand
miles.
Millions
were lost.
The Gulf
Stream was
our only
teacher
and a
bitter
one.

I
dreamed
of land
before
I saw it,
tasted
sweet
water
before
I met it
head on,
funnelled
up rivers,
slipping
into streams,
squirming
up brooks,
the snugger
the safer.
Every crack
that had
water to
breathe
was home
to me.

I
lodged
in a ditch
between
cool slabs
of peat.
I lay
like a warrior
in a tomb.
Time slept
at my side.
Catch me now,
you'll rue
the day. Old
eels won't
die. I knew
one chopped
into three-
inch chunks
but her jaws
still bit
the hand
that caught
her. Hah!
It's an
old tale
but I
like
it.

I
dream
these days
of green
light, a world
without walls
or floor. Wind,
rain tonight,
a full moon
and the air
is wet enough
to breathe.
This ditch
can't hold me
now. I'll steer
by the smell
of the sea. Land
creatures, if
you see me
coming, step
aside. I'm going
home. I warn
you. Don't
stand
in my
way.

Philip Gross

All the eels of Europe are spawned in the floating weed of the Sargasso Sea. They swim the Atlantic twice: once as young fish to reach our shores, and back at the end of their lives to spawn and die.

Yosemite*

She climbed a tree
and sang to the bears
while he bounced his name
back and forth across the valley.

He could make no sense
of the lunatic peaks
thrown together
in a conflict of geology

and closed his eyes
until it was evening
and shadows unfolded
a transient symmetry

that gave him comfort.
Then it grew dark
and she started humming
the one about the picnic.

Lavinia Greenlaw

*Yosemite National Park embraces a spectacular mountain region about 150 miles east of San Francisco, on the western slopes of the Sierra Nevada. It covers 1189 square miles.

The Buffalo of the North[*]

He stood, breathing in the resin scents,
his nostrils quivered and his wide hoof marks
tracked the mud; as Winter came,
he stood a statue of the dawn.
Head hanging low, horns tossed skyward,
silent in the little shadows of the octopus dark,
and the tramping elephant night, bigger than the sky.

His breath stained the huge mountains with frost,
and his horns locked with the sun,
and as he shook his head, his horns glowed like fire in the grey sky,
and as he impatiently pawed the earth,
the snow cataracted down and stung his hot hide.

And now he stands, breathing.
Head hanging down to the fluorescent snow-light
which had started as a little shadow and had formed,
                              elephant like, upon the earth.
And the Buffalo lies down upon the soil,
and turns to white, and grows to cover the pines,
and sleeps with the land; covered with snow.

Harriet Earis

[*]*In the Medicine Wheel of the American Indians, the Buffalo, Waboose, is the spirit*
keeper of winter

The Stars Streaming in the Sky

The stars streaming in the sky are my hair.
The round rim of the earth which you see
Binds my starry hair.

from the Creation Myth of the Wintu

On Looking into the
Grand Canyon

The Colorado chuckles –
Me, I'd laugh.
Knowing I was strong enough
To slice the world in half.

Richard Edwards

Dune Tune*

Running down them, slow
motion moon walk
sand sliding, a landslide
ahead of you, avalanche
benching down at the bottom
you dive down them, gliding
right into the sea
leaving two neat lines
tracks that deceive
with no trace of the terror
the tumble and plunge
the dipping and dropping
the slidingandglidingand
crying down, flying down
dreaming all winter
of sand scraping bare feet
the length of the sand dunes
right down to the beach
then the scramble back, slipping
sand gritty on thin legs
dusting a layer
against sweaty faces
over and over
through the long afternoon
till you lie in exhaustion
gasping and laughing
and hating to leave it
but knowing next year
you will start again, here
at the top.

Katie Campbell

*There is a huge sand dune in the rocky north shore of Canada's St Lawrence River.

Mooses

The goofy Moose, the walking house-frame,
is lost
In the forest. He bumps, he blunders, he stands.

With massy bony thoughts sticking out near his ears –
Reaching out palm upwards, to catch whatever might be
         falling from heaven –
He tries to think,
Leaning their huge weight
On the lectern of his front legs.

He can't find the world!
Where did it go? What does a world look like?
The Moose
Crashes on, and crashes into a lake, and stares at the
         mountain, and cries
"Where do I belong? This is no place!"

He turns and drags half the lake out after him
And charges the cackling underbrush –

He meets another Moose.
He stares, he thinks "It's only a mirror!"

"Where is the world?" he groans, "O my lost world!
And why am I so ugly?
And why am I so far away from my feet?"

He weeps.
Hopeless drops drip from his droopy lips.

The other Moose just stands there doing the same.

Two dopes of the deep woods.

Ted Hughes

ARCTIC REGIONS

AND FAREWELL...

The Gondoliers of Greenland

The Gondoliers of Greenland
Are the Grumpiest folk in the North.
Their canals melt on August the Second
And freeze up on August the Fourth.
In those two laborious glorious days
All their incomes must be made
And the rest of the year they wait listlessly
To ply their ridiculous trade.

Adrian Mitchell

Innuit Chant

There is joy in
Feeling the warmth
Come to the great world
And seeing the sun
Follow its old footprints
In the summer night.

There is fear in
Feeling the Cold
Come to the great world
And seeing the moon
– Now new moon now full moon –
Follow its old footprints
In the winter night.

Translated by Knud Rasmussen

Polar Night

I sail in a ship of stars
drifting on a sea of sleep
where thin white fishes,
barely alive,
simmer in the icy deep.

The creak of ice is my music,
raw songs torn from its throat.
A white bear
shakes his pelt at the moon:
his shadow paws my coat.

No matter where winter takes me
my crusty ship is doomed.
The bright stars crackle.
My fiery dreams sail on
to be consumed.

Irene Rawnsley

Farewell Song for the Anthropologists

You go and I stay.
You take my voice and my verses.
Wherever you go, my voice and my verses will go.
I'll stay here,
and my voice and my verses
who knows where they will go?

> *Composed for the German scholar Koesster by*
> *Chief Bluesnake of the Araucano Indians from Chile.*
> *Translated from the Spanish version by Roger Garfitt*

Acknowledgements

The compiler and publishers would like to thank the following for permission to use copyright material in this collection.

'Evening, Albufeira' by Moira Andrew by kind permission of the author; 'Mermaids' from *Scottish Nursery Rhymes*, ed. Norah and William Montgomerie, reprinted by permission of Chambers Publishers; 'The Stars Streaming in the Sky' by William Brandon by kind permission of the author; 'From the Loch' by Lois Beeson by kind permission of the author; 'In a Kenyan Garden' by Gerard Benson by kind permission of the author; 'Pods Pop and Grin' by James Berry from *When I Dance*, reprinted by permission of Hamish Hamilton Ltd; 'Dune Tune' by Katie Campbell by kind permission of the author; 'Out in the Desert' by Charles Causley from *Jack the Treacle Eater* published by Macmillan Children's Books and reprinted by permission of David Higham Associates; 'The Dancers' by Charles Causley from *Secret Destinations* published by Macmillan Children's Books and reprinted by permission of David Higham Associates; 'The Day of the Annual Firework Display' by John Coldwell by kind permission of the author; 'Lechwe' by Sue Cowling from *What is a Kumquat?* reprinted by permission of Faber and Faber Ltd; 'Carnival in Rio' by Fred D'Aguiar by kind permission of the author; 'The Bunyip' by James Devaney from *Earth Kindred* reprinted by permission of Angus & Robertson (Australia); 'Curandero', 'Grave of a Princess' and 'I Am Surma' by Gina Douthwaite by kind permission of the author; 'Breeze of Ghosts' by Helen Dunmore by kind permission of the author; 'The Buffalo of the North' and 'Mountain Peak' by Harriet Earis by kind permission of the author; 'On Looking into the Grand Canyon' by Richard Edwards from *The House That Caught Cold* reprinted by permission of Viking Books Ltd; 'In South Africa' by Helena Echlin from *Young Words* reprinted by permission of Macmillan Children's Books; 'Topkapi' by John Fuller from *The Beautiful Inventions* reprinted by permission of Secker and Warburg; 'Farewell Song for the Anthropologists', 'Seven Wishes' and 'The Song of Chief Koruinka' translated by Roger Garfitt, by kind permission of the author; 'Yosemite' by Lavinia Greenlaw from *The Cost of Getting Lost in*

Space reprinted by permission of Turret Books; 'Sargasso' by Philip
Gross by kind permission of the author; 'Giraffes' by Phoebe Hesketh
from *New and Collected Poems* reprinted by permission of
Enitharmon; 'Mooses' by Ted Hughes from *Under the North Star*
reprinted by permission of Faber & Faber; 'Drought' by Accabre
Huntley by kind permission of the author; 'Back Home' by Amryl
Johnson by kind permission of the author; 'Dancing the Anaconda' by
Mike Johnson by kind permission of the author; 'The Doll Festival' by
James Kirkup by kind permission of the author; 'A Harvest of Wheat'
by Tariq Latif by kind permission of the author; 'New Zealand Shore'
by Hilary Llewellyn-Williams by kind permission of the author; 'The
Coming' by E A Markham by kind permission of the author;
'Aardvark' and 'Durianimal' by Roger McGough from *An Imaginary
Menagerie* reprinted by permission of Viking Kestrel; 'Great Grey
Kangaroo' and 'Lions' by Robin Mellor by kind permission of the
author; 'The Gondaliers of Greenland' by Adrian Mitchell from *All
My Own Stuff* reprinted by permission of Simon & Schuster Young
Books; 'Once in a Lifetime - Snow' by Les Murray from *The
Weatherboard Cathedral* reprinted by permission of Angus and
Robertson (Australia); 'Pompeii' by Judith Nicholls from *Magic
Mirror* and 'Village School' by Judith Nicholls from *Midnight Forest*
reprinted by permission of Faber & Faber; 'A Boat's Mooring Ring at
Kallikratia' by Simon Pitt by kind permission of the author; 'Swallow
Tails at Combourg, Brittany' by Rodney Pybus by kind permission of
the author; 'Hine-ruhi' by Cecil Rajendra from *Lovers, Lunatics and
Lallang* reprinted by permission of Bogle Overture; 'In the High
Mountains' and 'Polar Night' by Irene Rawnsley by kind permission of
the author; 'Innuit Chant' translated by Knud Rasmussen by kind
permission of the author; 'Conjurer on Charles Bridge, Prague' by Ben
Rice by kind permission of the author; 'A Song for England' by
Andrew Salkey from *Caribbean Voices 2*, ed. John Figueroa, reprinted
by permission of Evans Brothers Ltd; 'Death by Sacher Torte' and 'St
Petersburg, April' by Elizabeth Seagar by kind permission of the
author; 'Skiing to Voikka' by Sheila Simmons by kind permission of
the author; 'Rhinoceros' by Matt Simpson by kind permission of the
author; 'The Not So Slow Loris' by Matthew Sweeney by kind
permission of the author; 'Day by Day I Float My Paper Boats' by
Rabindranath Tagore from *Collected Poems and Plays* reprinted by
permission of Macmillan Publishers; 'Ireland' by Jill Townsend by
kind permission of the author; 'Haiku Calendar: Southern Version' by
Barrie Wade by kind permission of the author; 'May Music in Castille'
by Ted Walker by kind permission of the author.

Index of titles

Index of authors